Ancient Gr

Contents

Find the Greek city-states of Athens and Sparta.

Name of letter	Greek letter	English letter	Name of letter	Greek letter	English letter
alpha	A	A	nu	N	N
beta	B	B	omicron	O	O
delta	Δ	D	pi	Π	P
epsilon	E	E	rho	P	R
phi	Φ	F	sigma	Σ	S
gamma	Γ	G	tau	T	T
iota	I	I	upsilon	Y	U
kappa	K	K	xi	Ξ	X
lambda	Λ	L	zeta	Z	Z
mu	M	M			

Some letters from the Greek alphabet are shown above. Which letters are the same in Greek and in English? Which are different?

3

Mount Olympus is the highest mountain in Greece. Ancient Greeks thought that gods lived at the top of Mount Olympus or in the air above it.

Zeus was king of the gods. He rode a chariot across the sky. When he made storms and threw thunderbolts at the earth, the Greeks thought they had made him angry.

Poseidon was the Greek god of the sea. He had a three-pronged spear called a trident. Sailors believed he used his trident to whip the sea into storms. They prayed to him for safe voyages.

Athena was the goddess of war. She was born out of the head of Zeus (left). The Greeks believed that anyone who looked at her shield would turn into stone.

Hermes was the messenger of the gods. He ran and flew very fast because his hat and sandals had wings. He was the god of science. The symbol for doctors today is shown on the left.

Athena, Hera, and Aphrodite asked Paris (on the right) which of them deserved the golden apple. His choice led to war between the Greeks and Troy.

The Trojan War was fought between the Greeks
and the Trojans. The warriors on the left are Greeks
defending their ship against Trojan warriors.

The Greeks gave the Trojans a huge wooden
horse. It was a trick! Some Greeks were hiding
inside the horse. At night they let other soldiers
into Troy. Then the Greeks conquered the city.

The Acropolis is a hill in Athens. On this hill Athenians built a temple to honor Athena. The temple is called the Parthenon. Its ruins can still be seen.

This drawing shows how the Parthenon may
have looked when it was first built. Compare
it to the photo on page 12 to see how different
it is today.

People who needed help from Athena prayed in her temple. They also sacrificed an animal on the altar in front of the Parthenon. Then they feasted on the animal they had sacrificed.

The gold coin on the left shows Nike, the Greek goddess of victory. The silver coin on the right shows an owl. The owl was a symbol of the goddess Athena.

Only men could be citizens of Athens. This citizen belonged to the Assembly. Citizens debated and voted in the Assembly.

Agora is the Greek word for "marketplace."
A person could buy food, clothing, furniture,
and other goods at the agora. Do you see the
Parthenon on the top of the hill?

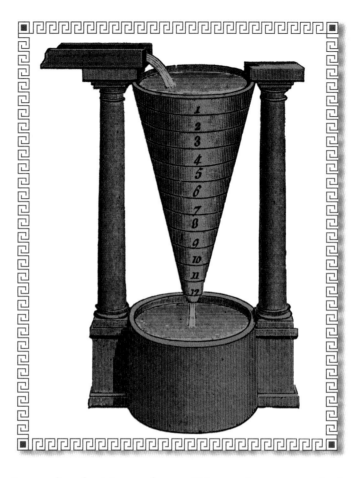

A water clock timed a citizen's speech in the
Assembly. A citizen could speak until all the
water in the clock had run out.

Citizens in Athens heard many speakers talk
about things that were important to their city.

In Athens, boys attended school. Sometimes they studied outdoors. They learned many subjects, including reading and music. Here they are using an abacus to help them learn math.

The Greeks liked to play and listen to music.
Students in Greek schools learned to play such
instruments as the lyre and the harp.

Girls in Greece did not go to school. They learned how to take care of a family and a home. They also played a game like our game of jacks.

Greek women had many duties. They were in charge of running the home. They also took care of the family. Cooking meals was an important part of their daily life.

Spartan boys learned to run, jump, box, and throw javelins. They had to be strong to become good soldiers.

A Greek warrior boards his chariot as he goes into battle. What might he be feeling?

Spartan girls kept in good shape by running. How is this different from the life of girls in Athens?

The ancient Greeks started the Olympic Games.
This photograph shows the opening ceremonies
of the 2000 Olympic Games in Sydney, Australia.

The ruins of the temple of Zeus are shown on the left. The other photo shows what the inside of the temple may have looked like.

Prizes were given to winners in the ancient Olympic Games. Which prize was for chariot racing? For horse racing? For running?

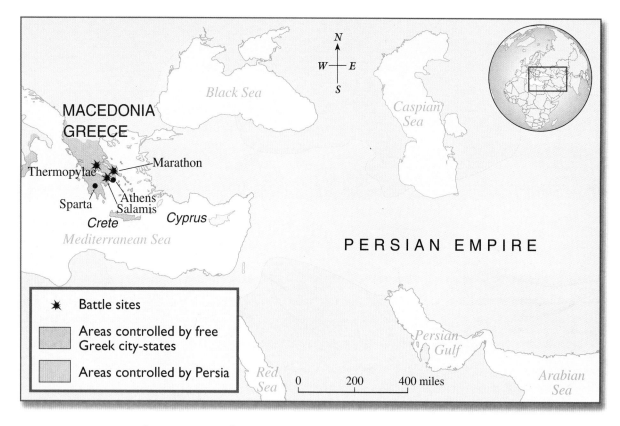

Persia was a huge empire compared to the Greek city-states.

Archers protected the king of Persia. The country now called Iran was once part of the Persian empire.

Soldiers used spears and shields in the battle
of Thermopylae. The Persians defeated the Greeks
in this battle. But the Greeks later won the war.
Find the warships in the background.

Leonidas was a king of Sparta. Today this statue of him stands in a Greek town.

The Greeks won a great victory over the
Persians in the battle of Salamis. After the
battle, the Persian navy sailed home.

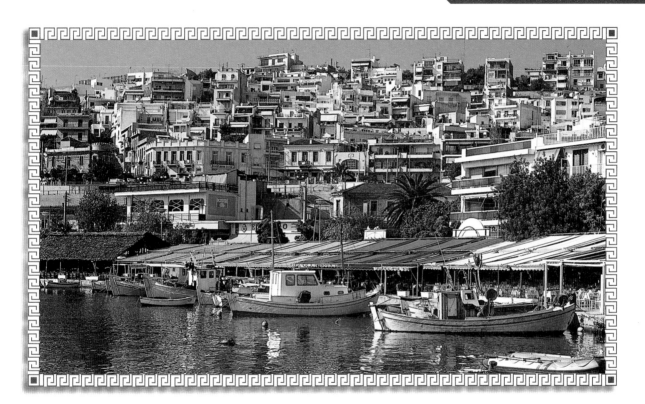

Ships from many parts of the world carried goods to and from Piraeus, the port of Athens. That port is still used today.

Pericles was a famous leader of Athens. He believed in democracy. He hoped that other Greek city-states would be democratic like Athens.

Plays were performed and festivals were held
in outdoor theaters in Greece. This photograph
shows the ruins of a Greek theater.

The citizens of Athens met in the Assembly. First they made speeches about important matters. Then the citizens voted.

Only men could be guests at a symposium, or dinner party, in Athens. Female performers played music at a symposium. This ancient Greek painting on a vase shows a symposium.

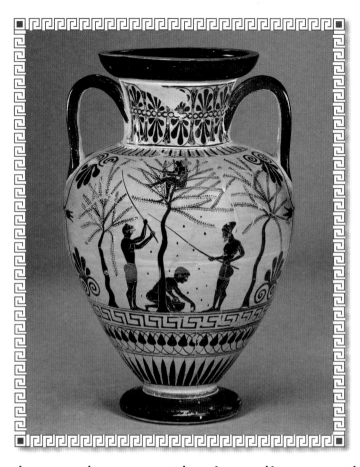

People are shown gathering olives on this
ancient Greek vase. Olive oil was one of the
most important products of ancient Greece.

The figures on this ancient Greek vase are painted in black on an orange background. The woman on the left is playing a reed instrument.

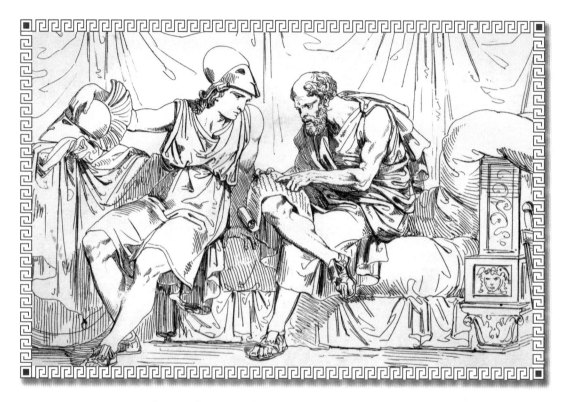

Socrates (on the right) was one of the most famous thinkers in ancient Greece. Here he is teaching one of his young friends.

The most famous student of Socrates was Plato.
This ancient painting shows Plato teaching his
students. Plato also wrote down things that
Socrates taught.

Aristotle (left) was a student of Plato. He was also a great teacher. Alexander the Great (right) was Aristotle's most famous student.

As a boy, Alexander tamed the horse Bucephalus.
Grown men could not ride the horse. But
Alexander rode this horse into many battles.

Alexander the Great became a famous military leader. He won many victories against the Persians. In this painting the Persian king runs from a battle. Can you see Alexander?

Troops from India rode elephants in battle.
Alexander moved his troops around until the
Indian king got tired of moving the elephants.

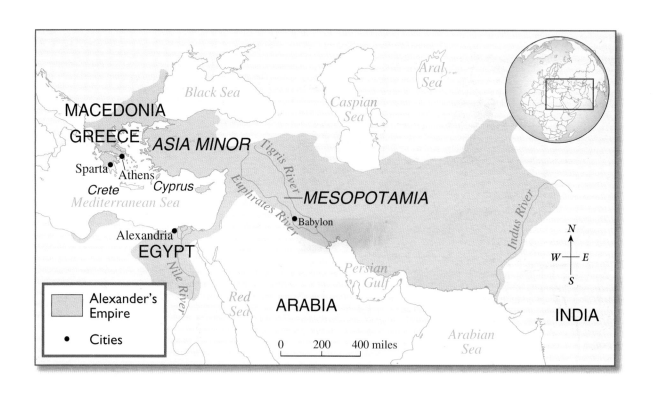

Alexander gained a great empire from his many victories. His huge empire is shown in purple on the map above.